W9-CEI-409

Ellis Island

ELAINE LANDAU

Children's Press®
A Division of Scholastic Inc.
New York   Toronto   London   Auckland   Sydney
Mexico City   New Delhi   Hong Kong
Danbury, Connecticut

Content Consultant

David R. Smith, PhD

Academic Adviser and Adjunct Assistant Professor of History

University of Michigan–Ann Arbor

Reading Consultant

Cecilia Minden-Cupp, PhD

Early Literacy Consultant and Author

Library of Congress Cataloging-in-Publication Data

Landau, Elaine.
 Ellis Island / by Elaine Landau.
     p. cm.—(A true book)
 Includes bibliographical references and index.
  ISBN-13: 978-0-531-12631-8 (lib. bdg.)   978-0-531-14781-8 (pbk.)
  ISBN-10: 0-531-12631-5 (lib. bdg.)   0-531-14781-9 (pbk.)
 1. Ellis Island Immigration Station (N.Y. and N.J.) 2. United
States—Emigration and immigration. I. Title. II. Series.
 JV6484.L36 2007
 304.8'73—dc22   2007011414

All rights reserved. Published in 2008 by Children's Press, an imprint of Scholastic Inc. Published simultaneously in Canada. Printed in the United States of America. SCHOLASTIC, CHILDREN'S PRESS, A TRUE BOOK, and associated logos are trademarks and/or registered trademarks of Scholastic Inc.

1 2 3 4 5 6 7 8 9 10 R 17 16 15 14 13 12 11 10 09 08

Find the Truth!

Everything you are about to read is true **except** for one of the sentences on this page.

Which one is **TRUE**?

T or F   Millions of people had their names changed on Ellis Island because inspectors could not understand them.

T or F   An immigrant could get sent back across the ocean for having an eye infection.

Find the answer in this book.

3

Contents

THE **BIG** TRUTH!

**The Ellis Island Immigration
Center opened on January 1, 1892.**

A family from Poland show their landing cards to enter the United States.

Photographs of immigrants and their relatives are displayed at the Ellis Island Immigration Museum.

Immigrants from around the world arrived in New York Harbor by ship. Someone standing at the southern tip of Manhattan could see the Statue of Liberty in the distance. Can you find it?

CHAPTER 1

The Immigrants

"There were probably as many reasons for coming to America as there were people who came."

–John F. Kennedy, *A Nation of Immigrants*

New York Harbor was a busy place 100 years ago. Ships came in from around the world. Some ships carried goods. Others carried something more special—**immigrants**. These men, women, and children came to start a new life in the land of opportunity.

7

Why Did They Come?

What drove people to leave their countries, homes, families, and friends to start fresh in a new land? Each immigrant's story was different. But many shared the same goals.

People came to escape poverty. Some barely had enough to eat. They wanted a chance to work for a better life. Others who were not so poor wanted to be better off. They had heard that with hard work, anyone could become rich in the United States.

Many immigrants were looking for freedom or safety. Some left countries that didn't allow the practice of certain religions. Others came from places where people could be jailed or even killed for opposing their government. They knew they could practice their own religion and believe what they wanted in the United States.

Fathers often came alone to the United States. They earned money to pay for their families' tickets. Then the families could follow. Here, a mother and her children arrive.

Immigrants to the West Coast came through Angel Island near San Francisco.

The first stop for many immigrants was a tiny island in New York City called Ellis Island. Here doctors and inspectors checked the new arrivals. These doctors and inspectors could admit immigrants into the United States. Or they could send them on a long journey back home.

People often came after years of planning. They sold everything they owned to buy their tickets. Sometimes there was only enough money for one or two tickets at a time. It could take years for an entire family to reach the United States.

Where Ellis Island Immigrants Came From

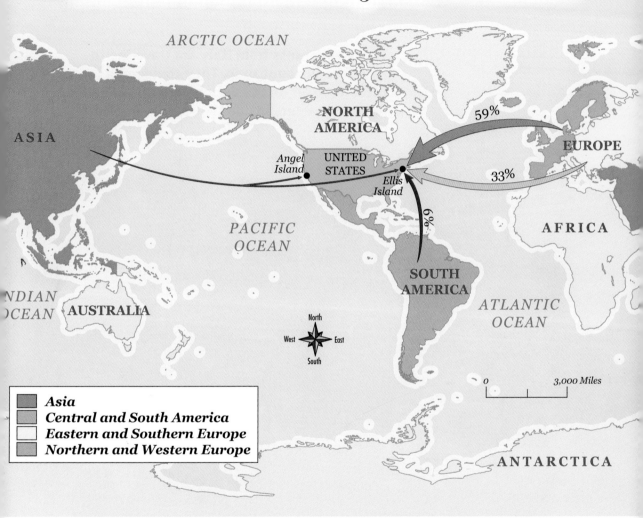

Asia
Central and South America
Eastern and Southern Europe
Northern and Western Europe

The arrows on this map show where the immigrants who arrived at
Ellis Island came from. Thicker arrows mean more immigrants came
from this area. Only 1 percent of Asian immigrants came through
Ellis Island.

These emigrants from Italy are traveling to New York in about 1900. They could get a little fresh air on the deck before returning to their quarters inside the ship.

CHAPTER 2

A Difficult Trip

On some trips to the United States, many passengers didn't survive.

Deciding to leave home was the first part of a long, hard journey. People who leave their country to live in a new place are called **emigrants**. Most emigrants came to the United States on **steamships**. The trip across the Atlantic Ocean was long, and most people did not travel in style.

Before Leaving

The first step was to buy a ticket for passage across the ocean on a ship. Many emigrants bought their tickets from salesmen who traveled from town to town throughout Europe. The cheapest tickets cost around $30. That would be more than $700 today. It was a huge purchase for someone who barely had money for food.

Many families in Europe struggled even to feed themselves during hard times. These Russian families wait in line for free food.

An emigrant in Finland bought this ticket to travel to the United States in 1896.

Until 1900, immigrants to the United States just needed a ticket. After 1900, they also needed a passport and a document called a **visa**. A visa gives someone permission to enter a country. U.S. offices located in other countries gave out visas.

After buying a ticket, people had to travel from their towns to a **port** city. A port city has a place for ships to dock. Many people walked with all their belongings. The lucky ones took a train to the ship. Still others rode on horseback or in a wagon.

In this illustration, emigrants to America
wait near the dock to board a ship.

Once they arrived at the port, emigrants had to wait days, weeks, or even months for the ship to arrive. Steamship companies often agreed to provide housing for ticket holders while they waited.

The steamship companies hired doctors to examine all the passengers. Any person with an illness was turned away. Emigrants were given shots to prevent disease. They often took disinfecting baths to kill germs. Only then were they allowed to board a ship.

Crossing the ocean to reach Ellis Island could take more than a month!

An ocean liner bringing immigrants to America anchors off the shore of Ellis Island.

Traveling in Steerage

Steerage was the area near the ship's bottom. It was close to the steering equipment. The cheapest tickets were in steerage. Passengers climbed down steep stairways to get there. As many as 2,000 passengers crowded together.

The steerage area was dark and unclean. There was little fresh air. There weren't enough washrooms either. The smell was hard to bear. Yet people were willing to travel this way to get to the United States.

The steerage section of a ship was crowded, dirty, and unpleasant.

The Steerage Class

Take a close look at life in the steerage section of a ship—if you can stand it.

- A passenger and his belongings had to fit in a narrow bunk.

Emigrants in steerage slept in narrow bunks with all their possessions.

- Mattresses were filled with straw or seaweed.

- Floors were often covered in dirt and vomit.

- As many as 300 passengers shared two bathrooms.

- Passengers ate small portions of bread, potatoes, and meat, scooped from large kettles.

- What did passengers do all day? They played cards, sang, danced, told stories, and practiced English.

By 1895, immigrants were flooding into America.
Here, weary travelers wait for permission to leave
Ellis Island to start their new lives as Americans.

CHAPTER 3

Why Ellis Island?

Tons of dirt and rock dug from subway tunnels were dumped onto Ellis Island to make it bigger.

The first immigrants to the United States came mostly from Europe. At first, they were attracted to the large open spaces. Later, they came to work in U.S. cities and factories. They were all looking for a better life.

Ellis Island is now a museum. More than two million people visit each year.

Most ships carrying immigrants to the United States came to New York Harbor. Immigrants went through a center in New York City called Castle Garden.

Huge numbers of people began to come after 1865. In time, it was clear that Castle Garden could not handle all the immigrants arriving in New York. The U.S. government decided to build something larger. The two-story Ellis Island Immigration Station opened on January 1, 1892.

Ellis Island Timeline

1892
The first immigrants come through Ellis Island.

1897
A fire destroys the wooden buildings on Ellis Island.

1900
Ellis Island reopens.

Fire!

A fire broke out on Ellis Island in 1897. The wooden buildings burned to the ground in just three hours. Fortunately, no one was killed. The workers and 200 immigrants escaped just in time. By 1900, a new and improved brick building had been built and was open for business.

Samuel Ellis, a New York merchant, bought the island in 1776 and named it after himself.

1954
Ellis Island closes for good as an entry point for immigrants.

1990
The Ellis Island Immigration Museum opens to the public.

Ellis
Island
Hospital

3.

3. Ellis Island Hospital

Sick immigrants were cared for at the hospital. Three hundred and fifty-three babies were born here.

0 ____ 400 feet

4. Stairs of Separation

Doctors watched immigrants as they climbed this staircase. They looked for signs of illness, such as sweating or shortness of breath. People with these signs had to have a more detailed checkup.

6.
4.
5.

5. Registry Room

Inspectors interviewed millions of immigrants in this room. Immigrants waited, often for hours, for their turn.

6. The Kissing Post

This was the last stop for new Americans. Here, they had reunions with relatives already living in America. There were lots of tears and kisses!

Getting Around the Island

★ **THE BIG TRUTH!** ★

Bridge to New Jersey

North / East / West / South (compass rose)

2. Cafeteria

Here immigrants had their best meal since leaving home. Some tasted ice cream for the first time.

1. Baggage and Dormitory Building

Immigrants left their heavy baggage in this building. They proceeded to dormitory bunk beds. The beds held immigrants who didn't have permission to leave the island yet.

Immigrant Building

New Ferry House

Kitchen, Restaurant, and Bath House

Power House

Baggage and Dormitory Building

Main Building

2.

1.

CHAPTER 4

On American Soil, at Last!

First- and second-class passengers usually did not have to go through an inspection at Ellis Island.

Reaching Ellis Island was a great moment for immigrants. But they still needed permission to enter the United States. For some, that would not be easy. Steerage passengers would have to go through a long immigration process.

Wealthy travelers usually went on quickly to New York City.

Getting Off the Boat

Steerage passengers waited for a doctor to board the ship. The doctors pulled aside people with illnesses that could spread to others on the island. Sick people who could be cured stayed at Ellis Island Hospital until they were better. Those who couldn't be cured were sent home on the next ship.

In all, about 2 percent of passengers had to return home. Many had little to go back to. Their dreams had been crushed in a day.

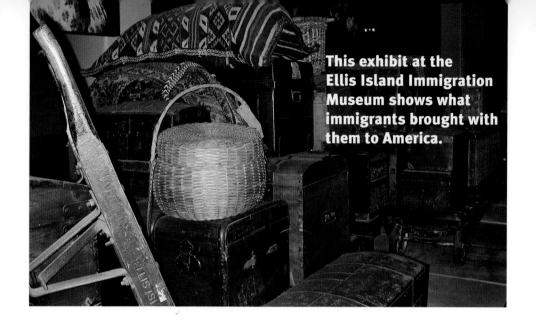

This exhibit at the Ellis Island Immigration Museum shows what immigrants brought with them to America.

The healthy immigrants went on to Ellis Island. Some compared the Main Building on Ellis Island to a castle. It was grander than anything most immigrants had ever seen. The immigrants entered the Main Building and dropped off their baggage.

The immigrants then climbed up the steep stairs to the second floor. A group of doctors stood at the top of the stairs, watching. If someone appeared ill or disabled, doctors marked the person's coat with blue chalk. Immigrants with marks had to undergo a full medical examination.

One of the most feared inspections was the eye inspection. In Europe, there was an eye infection that can cause blindness called **trachoma** (tra-KO-mah). Doctors wanted to prevent it from spreading to the United States. So they checked immigrants—by turning their eyelids inside out with a special hook.

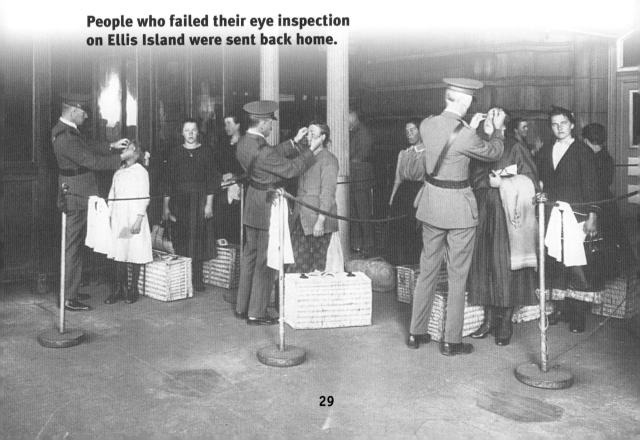

People who failed their eye inspection on Ellis Island were sent back home.

Immigrants waited for their turn in the Registry Room before answering questions.

One Ellis Island interpreter spoke 15 different languages!

U.S. immigration officials interview newcomers to America at Ellis Island in 1908.

The Legal Inspection

The next stop was the Registry Room. That's where immigrants had to answer questions from legal inspectors. These inspectors frightened many people. They wore suits, which made them look rich and important to the immigrants.

Next to the inspectors stood **interpreters**. They helped immigrants who didn't speak English. Most interpreters spoke about six languages. One Ellis Island myth says that immigration officials changed many people's names because they couldn't understand them. In fact, often interpreters who checked names spoke and read each immigrant's language.

Ellis Island officials checked each immigrant's documents.

The inspectors checked 29 pieces of information about each immigrant. Immigrants had to say how old they were, what jobs they could do, and if they were married. There were also questions about their personal beliefs concerning right and wrong, or **morals**. Inspectors wanted to identify any likely criminals.

A **literacy** test was added in 1917. All immigrants over 16 years of age had to prove they could read and write. Most read parts of the Bible aloud in their own language. Those who failed might be sent home.

Many immigrants practiced answering these questions during the long hours at sea. Although it was frightening, the legal inspection only took a few minutes. Most immigrants passed and got their landing cards, which officially allowed them to enter the country.

A family from Poland proudly hold out their landing cards for an inspector on Ellis Island.

A Longer Stay

After the legal inspection, immigrants walked down a flight of stairs. It was known as the Stairs of Separation. Immigrants with landing cards moved on to meet relatives or buy train tickets. Immigrants without landing cards went to the island's dormitories or hospital.

Entire families sometimes had to stay on Ellis Island for weeks or even months. Some waited for a relative to recover in the hospital. Others waited for relatives who had not yet been approved to enter the country. Five out of six of these immigrants were finally allowed into the United States.

Single women were not allowed to leave with a man who wasn't related to them.

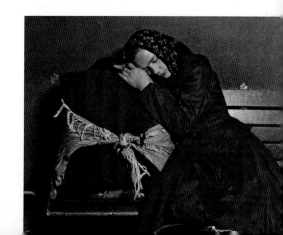

One Immigrant's Story

January 1, 1892, was opening day for Ellis Island. Officials waited to greet the first immigrant. Three ships carried 700 passengers. Who would be first?

That day was also the birthday of a young Irish girl named Annie Moore. The 15-year-old was the first person to step onto the dock that morning. She had traveled with her brothers all the way from Cork, Ireland. She was led into the Main Building and given a $10 gold piece. It was the most money she had ever owned. Annie's parents had arrived two years earlier. She would finally get to see them again, and show them her prize!

A bronze statue of Annie Moore stands on Ellis Island.

By the 1920s, fewer and fewer immigrants were let into the United States. Just a handful of immigrants stand in front of the Main Building on this quiet day in 1926.

CHAPTER 5

After Ellis Island

New immigration laws made it hard for people from Poland and other countries to enter the United States.

Here is the 1923 passport of a Polish immigrant.

For a time, Ellis Island was crowded and busy. But things began to change in the 1920s. Americans started having trouble finding jobs. Some blamed immigrants for taking too many of the jobs. Immigrants were blamed for other problems in the country, too. The United States became a less welcoming place.

Fewer and Fewer

Some Americans began to treat immigrants unfairly. They **discriminated** against immigrants from certain places, including eastern and southern Europe.

The U.S. government passed laws to limit immigration. The 1921 Emergency **Quota** Act set a fixed number, or quota, of immigrants. Each country could send only a certain number of people each year. The law's main purpose was to limit the flow of immigrants from eastern and southern Europe. Steamships packed with immigrants were turned away. This chart shows the act's effects on immigration.

Number of Immigrants Each Year		
	Before 1921 Act	**After 1921 Act**
From northern and western Europe	176,983	198,082
From other countries, mostly southern and eastern Europe	685,531	158,367

Americans have discriminated against different immigrants at different times in history. Workers at this 1879 meeting in San Francisco, California, protest against Chinese immigrant workers.

Anti-immigrant feelings continued to grow. Unfair laws were passed that kept out Jewish people and Catholics. (These laws were later changed.) The U.S. government lowered immigration quotas again in 1929.

By the 1950s, the immigration center on Ellis Island was no longer necessary. It shut down in 1954.

By the 1950s, only a few dozen immigrants were coming through Ellis Island each year. The government no longer needed the Ellis Island Immigration Station. It closed its doors in 1954. President Lyndon Johnson made it a national monument in 1965. But still the buildings lay deserted and began to fall apart.

In the 1980s, a group called the Statue of Liberty-Ellis Island Foundation worked hard to restore the buildings on Ellis Island. The Main Building reopened on September 10, 1990. It cost $160 million to repair.

It is now called the Ellis Island Immigration Museum. Two million people visit the museum each year. Its exhibits tell the story of U.S. immigration.

Visitors travel by ferry to the Ellis Island Immigration Museum.

More than 100 million Americans today have relatives who passed through Ellis Island. You may be one of them. These immigrants went through a lot to get here! They took a big risk for the promise of a better future. In the end, many found the American dream they were looking for. ★

Today, about 900,000 legal immigrants come to the United States every year.

More than 100 people from 44 different countries become U.S. citizens in a special ceremony on Ellis Island in 2004.

Years of operation: 1892 to 1954

Number of immigrants who came through: More than 12 million

Percentage who made it to mainland: 98

First immigrant: Annie Moore, age 15

Last immigrant: Norwegian merchant seaman Arne Peterssen

The most immigrants came from: Italy, more than 2.5 million

Nickname: The Island of Tears

Number of Americans today with relatives who came through: More than 100 million— that's 40 percent!

Did you find the truth?

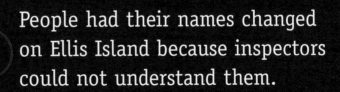

F People had their names changed on Ellis Island because inspectors could not understand them.

T An eye infection could send an immigrant back home.

Resources

Books

Binns, Tristan Boyer. *Ellis Island*. Chicago: Heinemann Library, 2002.

D'Amico, Joan. *The Coming to America Cookbook*. Hoboken, NJ: Wiley, 2005.

De Capua, Sarah. *How People Immigrate*. Danbury, CT: Children's Press, 2004.

DeGezelle, Terri. *Ellis Island*. Mankato, MN: Capstone Press, 2004.

Isaacs, Sally Senzell. *Life at Ellis Island*. Chicago: Heinemann Library, 2002.

Jango-Cohen, Judith. *Ellis Island*. Danbury, CT: Children's Press, 2005.

Klingel, Cynthia Fitterer. *Ellis Island*. Chanhassen, MN: Child's World, 2001.

Knowlton, Marylee. *Arriving at Ellis Island*. Milwaukee, WI: Gareth Stevens Publications, 2002.

Marcovitz, Hal. *Ellis Island*. Philadelphia: Mason Crest, 2003.

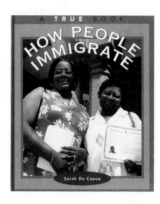

Organizations and Web Sites

Ellis Island National Monument

www.nps.gov/elis/

Read about Ellis Island and the Statue of Liberty National Monument, as well as the Ellis Island Junior Ranger Program.

Ellis Island Records

www.ellisislandimmigrants.org

Learn about Ellis Island history and search for families that came through the island.

Save Ellis Island

www.saveellisisland.org

Help restore the unused buildings on Ellis Island.

Places to Visit

Ellis Island Immigration Museum

National Park Service
Statue of Liberty National Monument and Ellis Island
New York, NY 10004
212-344-0996
www.ellisisland.com/

National Museum of American Jewish History

Independence Mall East
55 North 5th Street
Philadelphia, PA 19106-2197
215-923-3811
www.nmajh.org

Visit this museum to learn how Jews from Europe came to America, often through Ellis Island.

Important Words

discriminate – to treat people unfairly because of their race, religion, or nationality

emigrants – people who leave their country to live in a new place

immigrants – people who arrive to live in a new country

interpreters – people who translate speech from one language to another

literacy – the ability to read and write

morals – personal beliefs about right and wrong

port – a place for ships to dock

quota (KWOH-tuh) – a fixed number

steamships – ships powered by steam engines

trachoma (truh-KO-muh) – an eye infection that can cause blindness

visa – a document that gives someone permission to enter a country

Index

About the Author

Award-winning author Elaine Landau has written more than 300 books for children and young adults. She worked as a newspaper reporter, a children's book editor, and a youth services librarian before becoming a full-time writer.

Ms. Landau lives in Miami, Florida, with her husband and their son, Michael. She enjoys writing about history and often visits the places she writes about. You can visit her at her Web site: www.elainelandau.com.

PHOTOGRAPHS © 2008: Alamy Images/Mike Booth: 35; Art Resource, NY: 6 (Wurts Brothers/The New York Public Library), 31, 34, 36 (Lewis Wickes Hine/The New York Public Library), 22 right, 30 (Edwin Levick/The New York Public Library); Corbis Images: 7 (Louis Fabian Bachrach), 5 top left, 10, 20, 33 (Bettmann), 29 (Sy Seidman), 18 (Alfred Stieglitz/Christie's Images), 13, 14, 16, 17; Digital Railroad/Lee Foster: 5 bottom; Courtesy of The Ellis Island Immigration Museum: 23 left (Nick Cerulli), 4 bottom, 22 left, Getty Images: 42 (Stan Honda), 39 (MPI), cover (Roger Tully), back cover (Jeremy Woodhouse); Institute of Migration, Finland: 3, 15; Library of Congress: 5 top right, 9, 27, 40; National Park Service Collection: 32; North Wind Picture Archives: 19; Picture-History.com: 4 top, 37, 43; Robertstock.com: 21 (J. Irwin), 23 right, 41 (J. McGrail); Scholastic Library Publishing, Inc.: 44 bottom, 44 top; The Art Archive/Picture Desk/Culver Pictures: 12; Courtesy of The Statue of Liberty-Ellis Island Foundation, Inc., www.ellisisland.org/Daniel M. Lynch: 28.

MAPS by XNR Productions, Inc.